I0508830

This Book belongs to

____

____

____

www.ingramcontent.com/pod-product-compliance
Lightning Source LLC
Chambersburg PA
CBHW030707220526
45463CB00005B/1945
9781704606279